Sweep Away Your Thorny Childhood

Eight Steps
to
a
Life of
Well-Being

Sandra Elizabeth Clinger

Sandra

Learn to:
Heal Yourself
Calm Your Inner Child
Set Boundaries
Overcome Loneliness
Connect Deeply with Others
Free Yourself from Frustration and Abuse

#27

ISBN: 978-0-9892081-0-9
LCCN: Library of Congress Control Number: 2013906521

Images: Sandra Elizabeth Clinger
Copy Editing, Editing: Barbara Munson, Munson Communications

Scripture taken from The New King James Version ®. Copyright © 1982 by Thomas Nelson, Inc. Used by permission. All rights reserved.

This publication is meant for education purposes only. The author is not engaged in providing psychological, financial, legal or other professional services. Although every precaution has been taken in the preparation of this work, the author shall not have any liability to any person or entity with respect to any loss or damage caused or alleged to be caused directly or indirectly by the information contained in this book. If expert assistance or counseling is required, the services of a professional should be sought.

Trademarked names may appear throughout this book. Rather than use a trademark symbol with every occurrence of a trademarked name, names are used in an editorial fashion, with no intention of infringement of the respective owner's trademark.

"Nothing can bring you peace but yourself."

~ RALPH WALDO EMERSON

Contents

Introduction

Sweep Away Your Thorny Childhood is about redesigning, rebuilding and restoring your life. Each of eight exercises is an effort to recover and to heal your unique child-heart in this immediate physical world. The first time around, someone else built your life— your parents, most likely. They decided how your life would be. Yet, instead of thriving, many of us suffered from our upbringing. Instead of finding happiness and peace in our lives, we found anxiety, depression, loneliness and even abuse. For years, we carried that around like a load of bricks, not knowing how to fix things.

With this book, you have the tools to rebuild your life the way you want—and you can do it yourself. We *can* change our upbringing. We *can* re-erect our lives.

This is a step-by-step guidebook that uses simple strategies I learned to reinvent myself. It contains tools developed from my personal experience and collective wisdom that I called on to frame my life. These steps, specifications, worked for me and they continue to do so. I say they are simple because there is nothing in this book that is hard. The steps are grounded in common sense, logic, consensus, knowledge of spirituality and in particular my career as an interior designer. Since I have been involved in the residential construction business it was a short leap to seeing parallels between building a house and building a life.

Here is my plan for you: Whether it's a new home or a new you, you start with a concept plan, lay a stable foundation, erect a sturdy frame, raise a sheltering roof, adapt to environmental requirements, install a fence around your structure to retain your newly restored life, decorate, then open the door and let the light in.

Then, all that's left to do is take that proverbial broom and sweep away the remnants of your painful past, that thorny childhood that injured your child-heart. You will discover you now have a house with a fence around it that can shelter you the rest of your life.

To the Reader

How do I know this can work for you? So much of who we are is driven by our childhood. In my journal I described the nerve-wracking, saturated events in the tumultuous household of my formative years--disabling events that surfaced and re-surfaced throughout my adult life. I became depressed, anxious and frozen by self-doubt, guilt, shame and even the fear of success, bruised all over.

For decades I was mentally absorbed in repetitive attempts to satisfy and seek approval from a family of grievance collectors, recast grievances. I was driven by an oppressive mother, opening up again and again to her with hope in my child-heart.

I sought to validate and heal my overwhelming birth mother through appeasement and spiritual cures such as visiting holy shrines for her benefit. And, like millions of people before me, I tried to reorganize my troubled family through the study of psychology. I received a BA in Psychology with a concentration in abnormal development. For several years thereafter I worked with the developmentally disabled before moving on to other career choices.

It didn't end there. My formative childhood years re-manifested throughout my adult life as hypersensitivity. I engaged in non-stop mental preoccupation focused on my family of origin's tapes spinning in my head. I was ever busy in restless perfectionism, exhausting myself with hard driving over-performance. Top this with depression, chronic insomnia (designed to ward off the mother of origin's death threats) and jaw-clenching apprehension/hyper-vigilance. You would think I was on steroids!

I wasn't. But I was perpetually anticipating unknown dreaded events.

I developed a heart arrhythmia. I hosted the black pipe of sadness throughout my lean body. To this day I endure the startle-response of a toddler and the sensitivity of a new widow.

BUT--I did not want to be a "tragedy-ann." That was not the mountain my resolute heart would die upon. I wanted well-being, emotional freedom, happiness, balance, fun, contentment and a strong, purposeful life.

I defined, re-defined and constructed a good life in a very deliberate manner. And, after years of effort, I am exactly where I want to be.

Education and counseling formed a bulwark for my survival. They helped me extract myself from my origins and redefined my true self. Senior teachers and counselors re-directed and fortified me. I am deeply grateful for the professional constancy, love and care offered by my expert guides. They were my friends and my teachers. They were alternative caregivers, very able caregivers. Most people do not have access to this avenue of care. So this is what I propose for you:

Do it yourself.

I bear a need to heal others and be healed, so I have a purpose in offering my experience through this workbook. That purpose is to help others alleviate a mountain of pain, the pain initiated in the open-hearted formative childhood years.

I want to open a window for others, to offer back the hope of the tender child within, to enhance self-esteem, and to advance personal growth and well-being for those most in need.

Your adult child heart is an open heart still easily wounded. The orphaned aspects of your adult child need tools to end cycles of child-like repetitive behavior leading to poor life choices.

Using this book

This book offers you tools to end malignant cycles; it's a quick read, with exercises grounded in logic, collective wisdom and my personal experience. This is your unique workbook. It provides help to overcome anxiety and depression, to master chaos, and ultimately to avoid loneliness. It offers a pathway to health, comfort and security. It condenses basic disciplines and perspectives into an easy-to-follow application: a guide on framing your life. You will be asked to write brief thoughts and details of your life as you go along.

As an interior designer I could plainly see that others need to design their lives internally, as well as externally. I use the analogy of residential construction. Healthy, wholesome skill sets are defined as foundation, roof, fence and the like. They are familiar concepts for the reader to grasp and retain. Build a house that represents your intangible life skills. Design your life and restore your life through self construction, I urge. Then build a fence to retain and fortify your restored life.

The concepts contained in this book are not unique, but they are written from the heart and they are designed to be easily managed and successfully embraced. At the conclusion, you will have the insights to never be a tragedy-ann or andy.

You can educate yourself into well-being and you can educate yourself to happiness. You can overcome a heavy heart. You can overcome anxiety, depression and loneliness and replace unwanted feelings with a light heart, with love, contentment, satisfaction and felicity. This simple non-technical book will give you that perspective. It will make a difference in your life.

I promise this book will give you a chance to re-start your life. This book was written for you. Read the exercises and tips in no particular order. Try some of them to frame your day-to-day activities.

Work at it.
Just do it.
Put in the effort and welcome the results.
If I can heal, so can you.

You *can* create the life you want--a wholesome life free from psychological pain, graced by love, with pleasure in acceptance and understanding.

For a life lived with artful intention, read on and give up pain forever.

To your well-being,

Sandra Elizabeth Clinger

This is my promise:

You can survive a thorny childhood.

SWEEP IT AWAY.

Chapter 1

The Concept Plan

Design Your Future.

What is well-being? Consider this definition:

A healthy, peaceful life with good relationships
And enough resources to be able to be a blessing
to others.
~ JOEL OSTEEN
AMERICAN AUTHOR AND
TELEVANGELIST

You feel like the tower of Pisa, a leaning structure, so how do you get to well-being from here?

I will tell you how, straight out, that with or without a therapist, with or without a group, with or without a religion, no one and nothing will come along and save you, because there is no wizard, no expert and no wiz-kid. There is no quick fix, no magic pill.

You must do it for yourself.

Sorry.

So sorry! This is not OZ.

There is no other way.

Prepare yourself to
Do-It-Yourself

Say this to yourself:

There...is...no...wizard!

Shout it out loud:

THERE IS NO WIZ-KID!

Your future happiness depends on you.

Your future happiness depends on how you arrange and re-arrange your life, how you design your life for you.

You have the advantage. You are an adult now.

From this day forward, you can help yourself in ways you could not help yourself as a young child.

YES!

Your notion of self is no longer dependent on others, particularly the others, or perhaps those others from your childhood.

YES!

Say this out loud:

My future happiness depends on ME.

Free yourself from old repetitive compulsions to resolve any formative childhood difficulties. Be deliberate in everything you do.

Out loud, say this:
I can liberate MYSELF.

Do not allow family relationships from your formative years to define you today.

Do not be a passive victim. This is not where life rests for you.

Start this very day:
>Be deliberate.

Be deliberate in everything you do.

If your heart has undergone dismembering, know that it is not destroyed. You can work from the *big healthy pieces* still left in your tender child-heart. Your child-heart is an *able* heart. Find them-those big healthy pieces--and use them to heal yourself.

Heal the precious little child you carry deep inside you. Heal your *broken self* by using the intact elements of your *strong self.* Work from the unbroken parts of your being to heal your old wounds.

> *Strengthen the hands which*
> *hang down, and the feeble knees,*
> *and make straight paths for your feet,*
> *so that what is lame may not be*
> *dislocated, but rather be healed.*
> ~ HEBREWS 12:12, 13

>"...be healed."

There it is.
You have it on Authority.
>You can "be healed."

From this point forward, your life may require a leap, perhaps a radical leap, from all you have ever known and learned. You are on your adult journey now, your very own personal mystery journey. Access that journey and embrace it.

How will you know your way? Well, none of us were born with a road map. We had to learn our way. None of us was born with all the tools. We had to select our gear and use it as needed.

You will know as you go.

You will know.

As we go through this workbook follow your intuition.

Develop deep intuition.

Develop intuition in the form of personal radar detectors and sensors that monitor your immediate physical world. Detect, locate and track down what is good for you.

Seek out goodness.
Bathe yourself in decency, kindness and honesty.

Goodness will heal the aching adult child-heart deep inside you.

Embrace the uncertainty in your heart.
Have courage, dear child.

Be brave and grasp any fear as you face the uncertain future.

Think clearly and act well in spite of uncertainty.

By using this workbook you will replace anxious uncertainty with surety and with dependability. (Think of uncertainty, think of anxiety as a down payment on a debt that you may never owe.)

Erase it.

Erase anxiety.

Erase uncertainty from your heart.

Erase uncertainty from your concept plan, from your plan of operation, from your course of action, from characteristics of your future.

Whatever you do, don't become a tragedy-ann.
Don't die on their mountain! Promise me.

I honestly believe that everyone can recover from weak, thorny parenting;

Everyone can recover from a mixed-up family life.

It doesn't matter where you came from.
It only matters where you are going.
~ CONDOLEEZZA RICE
AMERICAN POLITICAL SCIENTIST AND DIPLOMAT

Enough said. Step in. Take over. This is your workbook now.

Let's look at uncertainty. Let's look at anxiety:

List three immediate fears, right here:

_____

_____

_____

That's enough.

Erase those fears from your Concept Plan.

All three fears—off-plan, off your concept plan. Don't revisit them. Do not analyze them. Pack them into a balloon and let them float away. We will build your new well-being on a sturdy new physical foundation.

You no longer come to your notion of self-hood through others.
You are not who they called you out to be.
You no longer are a reflection of those others.
You make your own choices now on your own.
Equip yourself with a fresh, new definition of self:

Redefine your lifestyle.

Redefine your future.

Redefine yourself.

Define yourself.

If we could first know where we are,
and whither we are tending,
we could better judge what to do,
and how to do it.
~ ABRAHAM LINCOLN
16TH PRESIDENT OF THE UNITED STATES

It is possible.

Now keep your singular goal in mind:
Well-being

Do it. Do some of it. I urge you.

This is your Concept Plan:

Feel contentment.
Feel security.
Feel comfort.
Enjoy good health.
Live in peace.
Bless others with your life.

To experience well-being with the big "W"

Weave in Spirit.

Weave Spirit into everything you do.

Spirit is your life-force, your essence. It is your nature as it connects to deity.

Any nature without God will cave from within.

You are connected to God whether or not you are aware, whether or not you feel connected to God—at this very physical moment.

I know the plans I have for you,
plans for peace,
and a future full of hope.
~ JEREMIAH 29

God loves us with the big "L." We are God's beautiful children. God gave life to us.

God did not put us on this earth to be miserable and fail. God put us on this earth to be happy and to succeed, to be embraced by love, to love and be loved.

Blessed is the nation whose God is the Lord.
and the people whom He has chosen
as His own inheritance.
~ PSALMS 33:12

I am convinced human life is the core gift from God.

This is the gift!

Every day of life is a gift. This colorful world is a gift.

Accept the gift and enjoy it fully. Enjoy it today.

In gratitude to God, lay a sturdy foundation for a really good life for yourself and for everyone around you. Start today! You have it coming, a really good life that is. You deserve a good life. And equally important, those around you will benefit from your well-being.

It's OK to be sad.

It is even OK to be sorrowful.
Emotional orphans, like us, have an advantage. Our sorrowful past allows us to be in close compassion and empathy with others who suffer and grieve. Compassion is a measure of our singular humanity, and the exercise of compassion is an ultimate human goal.

Your concept plan: To put your concept plan in action, to design your future—your happiness—it may depend on how you

Arrange,
Then
Re-arrange,
Your brain.

Human beings, by changing the inner attitudes of their minds,
can change the outer aspects of their lives.
~ WILLIAM JAMES
AMERICAN PHILOSOPHER AND PSYCHOLOGIST

The brain[1] is constantly rewiring itself. You **can** change your brain; you can train your brain—because it is **your** brain. Your brain is your very own frontier.

Own it.

Embrace it.

Make your brain work for you:

Your beliefs become your thoughts.
Your thoughts become your words.
Your words become your actions.
Your actions become your habits.
Your habits become your values.
Your values become your destiny.
~ MAHATMA GANDHI
PREEMINENT LEADER OF INDIAN NATIONALISM

Your mind, the way you perceive yourself and the way you perceive the world, can change.
Your perception can change your behavior. And as your behavior changes, your life will change.

Write down what well-being looks like for you, what you envision for your future, your dreams, and your goals. This will be your personal Concept Plan.

---

[1] Brain is wits.

Concept Plan Design Criterion:

Build something that can last.

Personal Concept Plan

Example: enjoy good relationships
Example: access appropriate resources
Example: learn healthy life skills

_____
_____
_____
_____
_____

Please read on.

You are worth it.

Forgiveness is not welcoming the abuser back into your life."
~ OPRAH WINFREY
AMERICAN MEDIA PROPRIETOR, TALK SHOW HOST, PHILANTHROPIST

Chapter 2

Lay a Stable Foundation

Build it on deep footers so the frost can't penetrate.

Start with your physical circumstance, reachable in this physical world.

Your physical condition can form an impenetrable and unshakeable base, a foundation for stability and for your personal growth. Think of footings, footers as caissons in residential construction. Think of them as columns, piers, anchors, that hold your life in place and support the weight.[2] They are your footprint. These footers will sustain you.

One caution before you dig:
Seek professional help, the best help you can afford.

You may benefit from either talking about yourself individually or in a professionally directed group. If you choose the group experience, then locate a *safe* group to join, a reinforcing group, a tender group that accepts possible collapses, voids and sink holes.

Get the very best help that is accessible to you.

---

[2] Each of us will need more or fewer footers, depending upon the depth of penetration required. Develop only what you need and deep enough to go below the frost line.

Footer 1: Assess your assets. Identify your positive self. Assess your physical and mental strengths, your internal and external assets. This is an inventory of who you really are. You have many positive assets, so write them down and organize them in their order of strength.

Bank on those assets as reinforcement to carry you through anything that may come upon you. Write down ten assets in order of strength.

Personal Asset Inventory

Example: good health
Example: keen mind

_____

_____

_____

_____

_____

One extra for added support:

_____

This list is you. This is your **Personal Asset Inventory**. It lets you know you, the real you, the positive you, not some outsider's definition of who you are. Wow!

You found your strength. And what strength!

Read your Personal List of Assets out loud. Share it with others. This is a deep footer. Your assets will carry the load. Expand your asset list from time to time to ensure extra strength, for good measure.

Acknowledge your liabilities, acknowledge your vulnerabilities, if you must, but focus on your strengths. Liabilities and vulnerabilities are like sloping ground that may require an additional caisson or two. These are step-down caissons, to maintain a level foundation. Identify a step-down asset, to offset a liability or vulnerability, just one more for good measure, in case the ground is soft.

One Step-down Asset

_____

Footer 2: Avoid fr-enemies. Avoid friends who are really enemies undermining you and undermining your well-being. You do not need even one frenemy, a relationship that fails you and creates stress. Seek out caring, healing, feeling people, supportive relationships. Compassionate relationships can relieve stress. Warning, strong warning: Stay away from predators.

Do you have predators or a frenemy in your life?

Acknowledge any frenemy:

_____

_____

Decide what you want to do. Distance is a valuable tool. Just recognizing the relationship as non-supportive is also a valuable tool.

Footer 3: Practice self-care. Vow to take care of yourself. Today you have value. In your past you may have been nobody's child, but today you are the parent of your own inner child. Note this: self-care is like a concrete crib; it's a retaining wall for life. It assists you in caring for the precious little child inside you. Promise today: I will take care of myself.

Personal Self-Care List

_____

_____

_____

_____

Footer 4: Engage fully in body care. Invest in an artisan body. Be responsible for that inner child in you, right now, by taking care of your unique one-of-a-kind body. Adjust it. Re-craft it, if necessary. Identify body-care goals.

Body-Care Goals

_____

_____

_____

_____

_____

Footer 5: Stand up. Control your posture. Think of yourself as a dowel or a steel billet. Stand tall—head over heart, shoulders back and down. Stretch up. Physically this is important to your well-being, to your health.

This is an additional vertical reinforcement of your true self, and a clear demonstration of your firm foundation.

Don't lead with your head.

Head over heart at all times, sitting or standing. It's OK to maintain a slight forward tilt. This is powerful. (Theater actors are trained to do this.) Be eager, be dynamic, be enthusiastic and forward-leaning in your body language.

Lead with your sternum.

Footer 6: Practice good grooming. Grooming is like foundation backfill and grading. Be well-graded, level at all times. Maintain your physical well-being through a very high level of self-care. Engage in daily grooming rituals:

> Don't ever go to bed without brushing your teeth.
> Wash your face every evening; and rinse your face with fresh water every morning.
> Always wear clean clothes.
> Comb your hair.
> Be fresh.
> Be clean; be spotless.

Dressing well is a matter of politeness. Wear your appropriate best out of respect for yourself and out of respect for others.

Good grooming is a baseline standard; it may be a safety factor too.[3]

Footer 7: Maintain a care schedule. Maintain an appropriate medical and personal care schedule with all regular check-ups. Good health acts as a stop, a membrane to prevent unwanted penetrations. Good health acts as a membrane that is a waterproofing beneath you.

> Get your teeth cleaned and repaired regularly.
> Have your eyes checked.
> Visit a health fair for a series of check-ups.

I know, I know. There are so many things to do. But don't miss one check-up, not even one.

---

[3] Cleanliness may prevent some illness/disease.

Do you need to make an appointment? Make it-now.

Can't afford it? Go to a school. Get your teeth cleaned at a dental school. Get your hair cut at a beauty school, etc. Attend a free health fair.

You know where to go. You know what to do.

Create a medical check-ups and personal care schedule here.

Personal Care Schedule

_____

_____

_____

_____

_____

_____

Stay healthy.
Bank on your good health.

Footer 8: Nutrition. Take in a very high level of nutrition, the best you can afford. The consequences of poor eating habits may set the stage for disease risk later. Think of food as fuel. Think of food as medicine. Eat whole food in its original form whenever possible.

Avoid processed food.
No junk food.

Make healthy selections, proper food choices, such as, fresh/frozen vegetables, whole fruit, meat, eggs, dairy and nuts.

Ask yourself throughout the day, have I fed my inner child today? Have I fed my deserving inner-child *well*? Have I fed my inner-child nutritiously?

For he who eats or drinks in an unworthy manner eats and drinks judgment to himself, not discerning the Lord's body.
~ 1CORINTHIANS 11:29

List your food and beverage selections for tomorrow— anticipate them. And write a list of foods to avoid.

Tomorrow's Food	Foods to Avoid
_____	Chemical additives (Eee!)
_____	High-fructose corn syrup (Yuk!)
_____	Sugary food (Yuk! Yuk!)
_____	_____
_____	_____
_____	_____

Drink water.
Drink plenty of water.
For nutritional supplements, keep it simple—not too many tablets and capsules. Keep it simple.

Footer 9: Exercise six days per week. No, not six days, exercise *every day*. Take a walk. *Do something* physical every day. Exercise in every little thing you do.

Make the extra physical effort in everything you do throughout your day. Do not be physically passive, sluggish or lazy like a stagnant pond. Initiate action from inside out.

Be physically proactive.

19

Footer 10: Daily check list. Check before bedtime. You are the parent of your deserving inner child now, so check yourself that you are taking the utmost care of your inner child. Review the positive aspects of your day in your mind.

Each night before sleep, ask yourself: *did I take excellent care of my inner child today? Did I embrace my inner child?* Consider your positive bedtime review as the final day's punch list. This review reinforces certainty in your life. Thank God and the good people around you for all the good in your day. Now go to sleep.

Footer 11: Sleep is a cure. It is good practice for any foundation to have time to cure, to set-up, before adding weight and unbearable stressors. So get plenty of sleep, seven hours minimum, eight if you can. Take naps, re-charge, 20-30 minutes, in a dark room, if possible. Lie down.

Be still and know that I am God.
~ PSALMS 46:10

What a great meditation for rest! What a great meditation for a recharge!

Identify the elements of your personal re-charge. What can you do to recharge your body and your mind?

Recharge, Replenish and Renew

Regenerate
Example: stretch muscles

_____

Restore
Example: drink more water

_____

20

Rebuild
Example: watch my food intake

_____

_____

Repair
Example: 20 minute walk outside

_____

_____

_____

Footer 12: Protect yourself. Practice self-preservation.

Safety check:
Are you safe?
Are your surroundings safe?

Check out your environment.
Look up.
Look around.
Be aware at all times.
Be vigorous and be proactive about your everyday safety.
Be attentive.

Get safe and stay safe. Safety is your right as a human being.

> *"I will set him in the safety for which he yearns."*
> ~ PSALMS 12:5

Footer 13: Avoid risk. Avoid physical risk. Avoid economic risk. Challenge yourself, appropriately, but stay out of harm's way at all times.

Avoid the cliff of unnecessary risk-taking.

Footer 14: Avoid dangerous people. We considered frenemies early in this effort. Over and above avoid anyone who may physically, emotionally, mentally, financially or morally impair you.

You will know them by their fruits.
~ MATTHEW 7:16

If you are uncertain, get verification.

Ask questions.
Ask the right questions.
Be alert.
Notice unsuitable behavior.

There are warning signs, markers that act like an open excavation, like a sink hole. Any *one* of them can collapse your foundation. Follow your intuition, your inner truth, and notice early warning signs.

Notable Markers

- Intense anger
- Violence
- Disorganization to the point of deterioration
- Mistaken notions of persecution
- Discipline problems and non-compliance with everyday rules
- Inappropriate behavior: weird or frightening
- Police contact
- Drug use
- Propensity for risk taking
- Expressed fixation on a single individual or object
- Excessive expression based on a belief
- Denunciation of others; contemptuousness of others

- ◆ Bizarre thoughts
- ◆ Hallucinations
- ◆ Dangerous fantasies
- ◆ Threats
- ◆ Delusions
- ◆ Deceptions
- ◆ Suicidal announcements and plans
- ◆ Self-concept as a loner; the language of a victim, a martyr or a hero
- ◆ Shallow emotions, unmoved, never displaying joy, compassion, empathy

Some markers are ticking time-bombs. At worst they may become dangerous.

> Consider the number of markers presented by one individual or a group.
> Consider the intensity of the markers presented.

At best they can put you on a steep grade, demanding the construction of continuous step-down footers to keep you level.

Footer 15: Avoid harmful substances. Avoid anything that may harm you. Of course, you must avoid illegal or addictive substances. You must avoid excessive alcohol, or any other forms of dangerous ingredients.[4]

> Be honest with yourself.
> Be honest with others.

It doesn't take that much to build a tight level foundation and to be OK.

---

[4] If you have alcoholic tendencies, seek help. For example, contact Alcoholics Anonymous.http://www.aa.org/

An old theater adage instructs us:

Just learn your lines.
And don't bump into the furniture.
~ ANCIENT THEATER ADAGE

But it absolutely requires the absence of harm, particularly self-harm. Drugs can act as a void lifting the grade under your sturdy foundation. Drugs/alcohol addiction will cause periodic heaving of your foundation. They will de-stabilize you.

Footer 16: Develop a healing home, a safe home. Use your home as a healing mass of self protection. It is a given that our environment is one factor that shapes us.

Environments we've built shape everyone's moods,
thoughts, emotions and the ways we move and act.
~ ROBERT LAMB HART
ARCHITECT

Do you live in a safe environment? Shelter your precious inner child inside a healthful, healing, supportive environment. You are the parent of your inner child now. Take prudent care of your inner child in a supportive environment.

Is your lifestyle and environment healthful? If not, move.

Better is a dry morsel with quietness,
Than a house full of feasting with strife.
~ PROVERBS 17:1

Footer 17: Develop a functional home. Keep a tidy clean residence. Think of housework as proper spacing of your foundation footers. Create a daily rhythm to your daily cleaning.

Pick up after yourself daily.

Perform daily household straightening efforts as a base for a harmonious and functional living space. As you straighten each day ask yourself, "Do I really need that?"

Reach for simple visual harmony.
Reach for function in every object you control.
Be ruthless about this.
Everything functional!

Vow to live simply.

Take inventory of your home.
Inventory your personal possessions.

Footer 18: Develop organization. The precious act of organizing is in itself a personal meditation.

Get the clutter out.

Out, out, annoying clutter!

Less stuff = less stress.

Stuff is not well-being.

What can you get rid of and not miss?

Can't let go? The problem is not your stuff; it's the stories inside your stuff. Let go of the stories and you can let go of the stuff.

Be a minimalist.
Keep accessories to a minimum.
Create negative space for the eye and the heart to rest.

Clean your kitchen and bathroom cabinets; clean your clothes closet at least twice a year.

25

Organization and cleanliness is one manifestation of your level of self-mastery and an additional demonstration of mastery of your immediate world. Organization puts you in control of your physical environment.

Don't know how to organize? Try a simple rule: all like-kind objects together, facing or laying in one direction. Think of spoons and cups—all spoons together, handles down; all cups facing one way. Stop laughing and do it! Discipline yourself to use spoons as a pattern for all organization.

Is this too hard to do?

You say you don't want to do it?

Do it anyway.

Get up.

Get going.

Let's get this done.

> *He who is slothful in his work*
> *is a brother to him who is a great*
> *destroyer.*
> ~ PROVERBS 18:9

Organization *stabilizes* your strong foundation. It levels you. It honors you with depth to carry the load. It offers you the experience of physical control in the physical world. Thereby it empowers you. It engenders self-satisfaction and enables you to see yourself as you truly are—without regard to miss-statements by others.

I always start with my seasonal closet: neat, clean, organized, all like-kind items together—facing one way.

You may take this one step further with all like-kind items, sorted by type, and further sorted by color, facing one way.

Whew!

And don't overlook your car: clean your car.

Clean your briefcase.

Clean your wallet.

Clean your purse.

If something isn't working, fix it. Leave nothing broken.

Never let anything get run down. It may break down when you need it the most.

Be efficient.

Be effective.

Put in the effort and welcome the depth of stability that organization provides.

Footer 19: Give away excess. No excess. Get rid of the excess in your life. It bogs you down. A good rule is: if you haven't used it in two years, you probably do not need it.

Do not collect, store, stock-up or hoard.

Ditch anything you haven't touched in the last year.

Throw away anything threadbare.

Unless you use it, toss it.

Return anything that can be recycled.

Organize retained items so you know where everything is—a place for everything, everything in its place.

Footer 20: Discover aesthetics. Aesthetics are enhancements. Enhance the spaces around you. After all, your home is a metaphor for you. Reach for a physically pleasing environment.

The aesthetic principle I embrace is
the design element of *harmony.*

Harmony is accord; harmony is pleasing; harmony is the perception that materials and objects belong together.

Carefully choose functional furniture, accessories and a color palette for soothing relaxation and healing. Reach for a blend, reach for accord in color, and look for similarity in shape, in form and in concept.

High-contrast or provocative high-impact, non-matching or intensive decorating will never serve us well. That is for others with higher thresholds for stimulation. Some of us are not good sensory gate-keepers. If it clashes or contrasts it will fire back at our tender brains.

Keep color and pattern to a minimum.

Leave some negative space in each room, blank areas with nothing on the walls or floor.

Even in a forest, nature develops negative space with a meadow, with a broad expanse on a hill or in low-lying grassland, independent of all other forest activity, a place for a deer to stand idle or graze.

If you are uncertain about your space then look outside, look to nature to guide you.

Design for calm. Select natural soothing colors, regional color from nature, and select materials from your current geographic environment. Avoid high contrast color that grabs attention.

Be geographically appropriate.
Live in indoor/outdoor environmental
accord.

Choose a color scheme from the following. Select a scheme and stay with your selection:

Analogous color: rich monochromatic color that avoids contrast.
Achromatic color: neutral color such as white, grays and blacks, soft degrees of brightness, sophisticated and safe as seen in fashion. Use natural neutrals such as glass, wood, and metal.

You have a stable, sturdy, firm foundation now.

You are neat,
You are clean,
You are organized.
You live in harmony and accord.
You live in safety avoiding crushing and crippling relationships.
Your personally crafted artisan body is well maintained through exercise, nutrition, sleep and a schedule of self-care.
You offer a pleasing presentation of yourself with good grooming.
You are employable.
You are datable.
You live in rhythmic accord.
You have self-respect.
You feel good about yourself.
You are confident.
You are proud.

Congratulations!

These intangibles are your frost-proof, level, sturdy underpinnings. This is basic work for a prosperous life of well-being.

This is a positive presentation of your cared-for inner self.

This is an exterior manifestation of situation control, of physical environmental control. This sturdy, stable foundation is your exterior manifestation of:

The peace within you,
The peace you yearn for,
The peace you offer to the world.
You are a calm sea now.
You are your own person.
No one made this new you.
The way you are today, you made yourself.

Keep working on it. Keep working at it.

Tribulation produces perseverance;
and perseverance, character; and character, hope.
Now hope does not disappoint,
because the love of God has been poured
out in our hearts by the Holy Spirit who
was given to us.
~ ROMANS 5:3, 5

Hope does not disappoint...

.

Chapter 3

Erect
a Robust
and
Sturdy Frame

Build a frame on a sturdy foundation for your life.

Every house needs a frame. You are ready to build your frame on your sturdy footers, the foundation for your life.

Look around you. You are no longer a leaning tower with an inadequate foundation on ground too soft to support you.

You have changed.

You have changed your brain, your wits, your understanding and your reason.

You are fresh.
You live in harmony.
You live in accord.
Your closets are clean!
You are organized and dependable.
You can count on yourself.
You can depend on your deep sturdy foundation.

We are ready to frame-up our house with some help from a sill plate. A sill plate, what is that? It's an interface. It fits over your footers and is tied to each footer anchor bolt.

The Sill Plate: Compartmentalize then isolate and divide. The past is over.

Your sill plate: I am not that anguished child now...never, ever, ever again.

Remind yourself,
> I am walking outside that old childhood.
> It happened.
> Yes, it happened.
> I acknowledge it.
> And it is over.
> The past is over.

Lay your sill plate down. Use it as an interface, over your foundation footers...all around. Anchor it to your footers. Think of your sill plate as a seal, a tight seal, a sorting seal, separating out the past and the present. Build on your sill with rim joists, all around. Your floor joists will tie to these rim joists.

The Rim Joists: Patience. Practice patience. Be patient with yourself. Check any tendency to be quick tempered and irritable, with yourself and others.

None of us were born knowing how to achieve well-being.

We had to learn it. We had to work on it. We had to develop the tools to acquire it. Accept yourself as you are today because you may not be ready just yet to *totally* get over your past.[5] Be patient with yourself.
You will get over it when you get over it.
Your heart will know when it is ready.

---

[5] Some of us spent a lifetime forgetting our story. Some of us need to remember. Sigh!

Lay a rim of patience on top of your sill. This is another interface.

Next, lay down one more interface. Build on your patient rim joists with a sole plate...

Sole plate: Self Respect. Respect yourself. Develop self-love. This is an outgrowth of patience. Grow in self-love.

Internalize your own speech to your own loving being. Try this: use soothing, sweet tones. Offer a loving atmosphere.

Be agreeable, be soft and pleasant. Do you love you? Yes, you do. Talk kindly to yourself and extend your loving self-speech to others.

> Look at others with loving eyes.
> Give warm greetings and farewells.

Try this for one day and notice how you feel.

Return to the Concept Plan: Show courtesy, friendliness, and consideration to everyone at all times, including your own self. Do not be rough, tough, vulgar or obscene, ever, even to a perceived enemy.

Don't cuss.
Slow down.
Take a step back and think of others.
Say thank you.
Respond: you're welcome.

Silence is sometimes
the best answer.
~ THE DALAI LAMA

Ask yourself what you can do to put others at ease. In the morning put a smile on your face. Wear it all day. Put a smile in your voice. Practice being an agreeable, pleasant human while you reach out to others.

> *Anxiety in the heart of man causes*
> *depression,*
> *but a good word makes it glad.*
> ~ PROVERBS 12:25

You are ready to go vertical now. Rise up walls employing the strength of full height corner beams.

Corner Beam 1: Never give up on yourself.
              Refuse to give up.

Overcome one obstacle after another. If another obstacle shows up, handle it.

Corner Beam 2: Define yourself to yourself. You know who you really are. Don't accept any reduction or any unattractive definition of you from others.[6]

Corner Beam 3: Be deliberate. We do what we do because we are the kind of creatures we are. Don't just go along. Cultivate a set of behaviors that are kind but deliberate. Be passionate about what you do. Love life and your ultimate passion will be life.

Corner Beam 4: Develop your integrity. Develop deep personal integrity. Integrity is an absolute necessity for your personal survival. Integrity will true up, straighten-up your walls. Keep them straight.

(Integrity is also your fire door.)

---

[6] As a personal example: my third grade teacher sent a note to my parents describing me as developmental disabled because *I couldn't cut using a school scissors on the lines.* This was true. The round-tipped scissors were designed for right-handed children. I am left-handed.

Live a good honorable honest life.
Then when you get older and think back,
you'll be able to enjoy it a second time.
~ THE DALAI LAMA

Adopt the attitudes and behaviors of those you most admire. Select a teacher, or select an icon—Mother Teresa, the Dalai Lama, Nelson Mandela, Clara Barton. Choose your role model on the basis of refinement and substance. Write down the role model you select:

Study your selected role model: Get to know your role model by learning more about that person.

Then, without being self-righteous, adhere to a very high level of moral principles—level, not sloping.

No slippery slopes allowed.
No buck-passing.
No ruthless excuses—ever again.

The silver-haired head is a crown of
glory, if it is found in the way of righteousness.
~ PROVERBS 16:31

Now lay down floor joists...for a firm footing.

Joist 1: Practice loving speech on others. Avoid crude, cruel or demeaning speech.

Our manner of speech conveys our innermost feelings, and vice versa.[7]
No cursing.
No bickering. Bickering hangs on people for hours.
Indulge in behaviors that express love.

---

[7] We're talking about style.

Be courteous.
Be patient.
Be kind.

The ways of a man's mouth are deep waters.
~ PROVERBS 18:4

Find your heart, the one you are putting back together. From the pieces of a yearning heart find your soft sweet voice.

Pleasant words are like a honeycomb,
sweetness to the soul and health to the
bones.
PROVERBS 16:24

Express yourself. Then, don't let anyone take your voice, your sweet voice, away from you ever again.
Avoid confrontation.

Even the most subtle confrontation is hostile.

A soft answer turns away wrath,
but a harsh word stirs up anger.
~ PROVERBS 15:1

Don't fight it out. Run from confrontation.

Joist 2: Don't worry. For heaven's sake, don't worry. Don't worry about things that are out of your control or not of your doing.

For example, you don't worry daily about a Yucatan-sized comet hitting the earth, do you? You don't worry on a daily basis about a world-wide eruption emanating from Yellowstone? Of course not! Both of these events are possible, but you set them aside; you offer them no focus-- as you should.

You don't take responsibility for something that happened in the sixteenth century; of course not. It is not of your doing, so you offer no focus.

Extend this don't-worry attitude to other areas of your life.

Neither do I concern myself with great matters,
nor with things too profound for me.
~ PSALMS 131:1

Be prepared, but...

Concern yourself over issues you do control, such as laziness, spending too much money on things you can't afford, eating bad food, eating/drinking too much, risking dangerous environments, carelessness, ignorance, dangerous action, and the like.

Joist 3: Develop inner calm. Be quiet. Be calm. Be still. Calm your inner child.

Pause 3—2—1.

Surely I have calmed and quieted my soul...
like a weaned child is my soul within me.
~ PSALMS 131:2

Smooth out any rough surface behavior and you will smooth out your very own being.

Find little pieces of your peaceful self. Put them together like a puzzle on a table. Fill in the pieces with more peace.

Now live in your quiet, undisturbed self. Be at peace, fully, from within. Remember a favorite meditation.

Be still, and know that I am God.
~ PSALMS 46:10

Joist 4: Plan ahead. Be deliberate. Think ahead, way, way ahead. This is life by design, life by concept plan, not life by default. Be careful in everything you do. Consider everything. Take inventory.

List your immediate plans for today:

_____

_____

Joist 5: Let go of the power struggle. Divest yourself of the power struggle. The struggle is/was not strength. Control is not strength. And it isn't fun anyway.

Let the power struggle go.

Note what you can let go today:

_____

_____

Joist 6: Pay attention to your inner knowing.

Value your insight.

Further that intuition, your insight, into healthful surroundings and the supportive intentions of others.

Joist 7: Open up your space. Don't fill up your space and time. Carefully note what is coming back to you.

If there is not much coming back then let go the one-way interaction; let go the non-supportive relationship.

Then drop back, fade out. Let it lose effect; disappear slowly into its own world. There may be no cause for this to go on.

Open up your space and your time.

Give yourself time to see what emerges out of that newly opened space. In open space you may learn what has meaning—in your life.

Joist 8: Reciprocity. Look for situations that are reciprocal. Do not invest in situations or individuals lacking reciprocity. Watch for inclinations to repeat past situations. Sharpen your skills. It's a matter of balance. Ask yourself, what is the return? You have a right to the return.

The return is the compliment and also the complement. The complement combines with you and completes you. It's a match. You deserve the complement. It combines well with you. It is the return on your investment.

Joist 9: Common sense: Act with common sense. What would Washington do? Not George, Martha! She was the CEO of a massive estate, a wise caretaker of her husband, a national heroine and a hostess. Martha had common sense.

Joist 10: Curb your oddities, your idiosyncrasies. Peculiarities are a turn-off. Accept your differences but do not expand on them. If you engage in quirky behavior, peculiar mannerisms or odd habits, or if you have an odd appearance, know that quirkiness may be unattractive to others. It does attract other quirky types which may not result in reciprocity.

Examples of quirky curbs
Never be late
Leave no messes
Be mannerly
Practice good etiquette
Adhere to the rules of good behavior

Examples peculiar to you:

_____

_____

_____

Locate the area of your life that leads to loss. Identify it. Call it out, and then get rid of it.

Joist 11: Prospect for opportunity. Allow opportunity to help you become who you are. Do not fear success.

It is safe to succeed.

Don't walk away from opportunity. When opportunity knocks, open the door and let it in.

Acknowledge favorable conditions. Find opportunity in favorable conditions. Don't stand still. Be a prospector and prospect for opportunity.

Joist 12: Be an achiever. Get things done. Self actualize! Make life happen. Time is limited. Don't waste time.

Wake up each morning and review what you want to achieve that day. Mentally prioritize your main tasks, and then proceed. Remind yourself of your priorities for the day. Carry them out. Do them.

A desire accomplished is sweet to the soul.
~ PROVERBS 13:19

Joist 13: Meditate. I don't mean practice a mantra. (Use a mantra if it suits you, of course.) But do bathe yourself in a thought, a useful, healthful thought.

For example, practice happiness as a path to well-being. See how happy you can be. Open up your heart and your soul to the world that God has given. Rejoice. Enjoy this world. Feel the pleasure in your existence. Draw happiness through your body into your core. Raise happiness from the soles of your feet through your body. Nurture your good fortune to be here. Nurture satisfaction.

Can't get there from here?
Get a broom.
Just sweep.

Clean up your mind as you sweep away dirt, dust, debris. Mindful sweeping enables concentration. Concentrate on a useful action.

Joist 14: Be results oriented. Open up to results. Open up to the outcome you get. If you don't get results, or you don't like the outcome, then your efforts may be misplaced.

Take this seriously, because misplaced effort leads to frustration and fatigue, and more poor life choices, as we already know. So try again with replacement efforts.

Joist 15: Be enthusiastic: in your voice, in your presentation, and in your heart. Enthusiasm is catchy. Enjoy yourself and be light. Be the light that illuminates others. Be bright and make all things possible. Let your own enthusiasm consume you.

Joist 16: Leave it up to God. God is light.

> *The name of the Lord is a strong tower;*
> *the righteous run to it and are safe.*
> ~ PSALMS 18:10

Your framework is strong and wide. Re-enforce it with cross bridging by reaching out to others. Tend to the needs of others. Examples are found in the first five works of mercy:

> *Feed the hungry;*
> *Give drink to the thirsty;*
> *Clothe the naked;*
> *Harbor the harbor-less;*
> *Visit the sick.*

This is a big house! Your house is cross-braced in support of others.

But what happens if your roof leaks? If you take away God and you take away nature—your roof will leak, you've made a mess of your decorating and sooner or later—there goes the foundation...

Let's raise a sheltering roof, together.

Chapter 4

Raise a Sheltering Roof

Tie it firmly
to
your durable frame.

Happiness and well-being require even more effort than unhappiness. Perhaps you were born into a rough world. Perhaps that world set up obstacles to your happiness. Perhaps you grew up too early. Perhaps you had to.

But today you have checked, inventoried, arranged, re-arranged your environment and your mind so your inner child can grow and be alone in harmony with your quiet adult self.

You created a safe harbor for your inner child.

You created your own definition of self. You cannot be invalidated—ever again. Within this safe harbor, within your harmonious environment, get to know yourself.

Raise-up your spirit. God is immediate.

When my father and my mother forsake me,
Then the Lord will take care of me.
~ PSALMS 27:10

Get to know God.
God is accessible.

Ask God to Enter Your Life.

For you are with me;
~ PSALMS 23:4

Hip Rafter 1: Step away. Compartmentalize your thoughts. You are not your circumstances or even your former circumstances.

The greatest part of our happiness depends on our disposition, not our circumstances.
~ MARTHA WASHINGTON
FIRST 1ST LADY OF THE UNITED STATES

Martha had experience, a lot of experience.

Walk outside the immediate events of your everyday life and consider difficult events in new terms: You are on your own now; you are on your own solid adventure. You are on a personal, singular spiritual journey. Compartmentalize your thoughts through the help of the Spirit.

Tie your roof hip rafter to your ridge beam.

The Ridge Beam: *Prayer.*
Align yourself with a very high spiritual purpose.
Address God in request.
Address God in thanksgiving.
Address God in praise.
Pray for faith.

Faith is the substance of things hoped for, the evidence of things not seen.
~ HEBREWS 11:1

Practice religion as a pathway, a route to the experience of God, if this is comforting.

Praise God in his sanctuary;
~ PSALMS 150:1

Science might be a pathway. Philosophy is another pathway. Nature is also a pathway to God. Many have found their path in the wilderness, in the wild.

We are all in some sense mountaineers,
and going to the wilderness is going home.
~ JOHN MUIR
AMERICAN NATURALIST AND AUTHOR

Select your route intelligently and commit to it.

What is your spiritual pathway? Name it here.

Spiritual Pathway

Hip Rafter 2: Compartmentalize even more. Mentally practice mindfulness, simply paying attention: When I am here, I am here. When I am not, I am not.

Banish the old-world voices in your head. Be here now, where you are. Stay in the present moment, right now.

Enjoy the now. Embrace it. Appreciate where you are.

Hip Rafter 3: Do no harm. Avoid counter-aggression of any kind in your voice, in your word choices, in your actions.

Hurling back words, striking back or confronting others increases collective rage, group rage.

This behavior develops interactive rage. Rage begets rage. It widens the separation between humans and cultures.

Stop a blow but never hit back. Never speak out, never threaten, intimidate, bully, menace, warn, or blame.

Be protective of your inner self. This may be a primary rule of survival.

Hip Rafter 4: No pushing. Control your anger. Dial down your responses. Pray "God deliver me from this hate."

Explaining The Ten Commandments, one young child said, "It means no pushing." The Commandments are a code of conduct among people.

No pushing.

Resolve to under- react.
Resolve to make the positive argument.

There it is—four hip rafters to hold up your ridge beam. Now fill in with roof rafters to further support your roof:

Roof Rafter 1: Collect yourself. Stay collected at all times. Calm yourself. Calm your inner child. Step aside.

Roof Rafter 2: Don't try to get even. Wait it out. Never, ever operate out of revenge. Do not act on vengeful impulses.

Repay no one evil for evil.
~ ROMANS 13:17

An ancient Roman general, noted for his revenge, explained to his troops; "Revenge is two graves deep." Indeed.

Step aside so you don't step into a grave that revenge digs for you. Even William Shakespeare warned us,

*Heat not a furnace for your foe so hot
that it do singe yourself.*
~ HENRY VIII
WILLIAM SHAKESPEARE

Others may say, what goes around, comes around. Don't count on it. It is my experience that in time, your nemesis, your opponent, will self-destruct; your unbeatable opponent will self-implode by virtue of a failed moral compass. Time arcs toward justice, so wait it out. Evil gets away with itself, in the short-term only.

*Let them be caught in the plots which they have
devised.*
~ PSALMS 10:2

Roof Rafter 3: Step outside any and all contentious events. Avoid conflict and do not accept the role of the "bad guy." Your new contemporary self is no longer the reflection of others. Get away from the other's reflection of you.

It is not you.
It was never "about you."
You are not to blame.

Instead say to yourself, it is not my fault; it is not my fault. Repeat after me:

It is not my fault.

Roof Rafter 4: If it's not your fault, then it is not your problem. How sweet. Separate out the things you can do something about from the things you cannot change. This is how—

If it *is* your problem, if it *is* of your doing, then you can do something about it, can't you? If you can do something about a negative situation, then you must.

Make a list of things you can correct

_____

_____

_____

> *God grant me the serenity*
> *To accept the things I cannot change*
> *Courage to change the things I can*
> *And the wisdom to know*
> *One from the other.*
> ~ SERENITY PRAYER, ATTRIBUTED TO
> REINHOLD NEIBUHR
> 1943

Make a statement about circumstances you are unable to correct:

_____

> *For every ailment under the sun*
> *There is a remedy or there is none;*
> *If there be one, try to find it;*
> *If there be none, never mind it.*
> ~ MOTHER GOOSE
> 1695

Roof Rafter 5: Never berate yourself. Free yourself from blame. Delete the old *mea culpa* button, my fault.

It is not your fault.
It was never your fault.

Roof Rafter 6: Acknowledge that some circumstances are just not resolvable. Some problems do not have a solution. Some problems do not have a resolution. This is vital information to understand and incorporate into our lives.

> *Some people get their kicks stomping on a dream.*[8]
> ~ FRANK SINATRA

---

[8] "That's Life" from the album *Sinatra Reprise: The Very Good Years,* songwriters: Kelly Gordon, Dean Kay.

Be determined to look good, feel good and not be miserable in the interim—and not make those around you miserable. It's your own feedback.

Roof Rafter 7: Don't try to change others. They are on a different spiritual journey. You cannot get to the gateway of their grief or to the gateway of their suffering. You can only heal your own grief.

Roof Rafter 8: Do not withdraw from others. We are members of the human community. Develop more friendships. Sweeten your life with friendship.

Reach out all day, every day.

The secret to friendship is showing up and being friendly. Make the extra moral effort. Be available. Listen, observe and participate.

> *A man who has friends must himself be friendly.*
> ~ PROVERBS 18:24

Roof Rafter 9: Develop more inner push. Become who you want to be--eternal recurrence is the test: would you be who you are today over and over and over again? This is your test.

Roof Rafter 10: Develop a career. Work gives life meaning. A career enhances work.

Do something you like. If you like it, it won't be just a job. Work it up into a passion. It will become a way of life.

One of the secrets to a good career, like friendship, is showing up. Listen, observe, participate and reach out.

Roof Rafter 11: Don't treat a career as a hobby. Do it, and do it well.

> If the road is rocky,
> If the road is rough,
> If the road is dangerous,
> Take another road.

Life is about your own individual path. It is a journey of discovery every day.

Roof Rafter 12: Find Your Core: Identify and define those non-negotiable values at your core. Start with the Ten Commandments. Identify two non-negotiable values in your life, for example, associating with healthy people.

Non-negotiable values

_____

_____

Twelve rafters! (You may even let your rafter tails show!)

You are ready for success. You designed your own concept plan. You installed deep stable footers. You framed secure corner beams and laid down firm joists. You raised a sheltering roof and tied it to your sound frame. Now we shall build a perimeter fence together.

But first stop and understand:

It may be necessary to do a little renovation. It may be necessary to gut parts to save the footers, to strengthen the corner beams, joists, and this roof you erected for yourself.

It is not
enough
to be beautiful
anymore.

You have to be well-run.

I wish I was an apple-cheeked peasant,
serving shoe-fly pie in Iowa.

Sigh! More work!

Chapter 5

Build for Adaptation

Adapt to environmental requirements.

Adapt with resilience to requirements.

I am not advocating suffering. I don't believe in the value of suffering. But suffering can be redeeming and unique. It offers the grace of a good challenge. It demands performance on a higher level.

Take note of the old psychoanalytic definition of depression, as an example.

Depression is anger, self directed.

Depression and suffering may in fact be the deep well, the opportunity, from which you reinvent and redefine yourself.

You are a jewel in a lotus blossom.
You are a perfect, beautiful, unsoiled creature.
Stand tall, shoulders back, walk out of the old mire.
Bathe off the old you and re-create yourself
into the person you want to be.
Feel good about yourself and your accomplishments.

You are your own best achievement. Give yourself renewed vigor. Give yourself a pat on the back, but then renovate/remodel yourself with renewed adaptation if necessary.

I experienced this example of adaptation on a trip to Chile:

Trout are not native to Chilean Patagonia. Around 1905 settlers from Hamburg, Germany introduced trout eggs to the southern regions of Chile. Since then a unique re-stocking has occurred. Chilean aqua-culture enables millions of escapees to swim to the sea and return each year to spawn in the unexplored canyons of their adopted rivers.

Some trout move into the Chilean river systems and stay. Nice for the fishermen but hard on trout.

The trout must work hard for a living. They do not live in slack waters. Their rivers contain little biomass, so trout eat terrestrials: grasshoppers, ants and dragonflies. They stalk their terrestrial prey.

I watched in awe one day as a fish hunted down its prey, flipped itself onto the grassy bank, captured the morsel and wiggled back into the lagoon. Surely these fish will grow limbs by the next millennium!

Adaptation and resilience!

It's this depth of adaptation, this level of self-repair and this magnitude of resilience that we may be asked to develop, even endure, throughout the balance of our lives. It takes moral courage.

One accessible tool for adaptation is nature. As humans we want and need nature. We crave it. There is integration between nature and humans that triggers well-being.

Nature is home for us.

Spiritual tools for adaptation are offered throughout philosophies and religions. They trigger well-being. The first four spiritual works of mercy are an example. They help create human health and well-being:

Bear wrongs patiently;
Forgive offences willingly;
Comfort the afflicted;
Pray for the living and the dead.

Chapter 6

Install
Solid Fence Posts

Fortify your life with a fence around it.

Your fence will surround your house. Think of an informal, open, natural looking fence. Install a post-and-rail perimeter fence to match your life. Read below, and then decide which posts will be your corner posts, which posts will be your end posts. Choose your posts to match your life.

Check-off four corner posts. Set them first. Be sure to anchor your corner posts and all end posts deeply enough to withstand the elements.

Select corner posts and end posts from the following:

Post 1: Count on today. Make the moment, this moment, every moment, count. Get pleasure from the present. Stay focused. Listen. Watch. What do you hear? What do you see? Look at life in all its dimensions. Think 3-D. Life has so much dimension—foreground, background and middle ground.

Today I saw a fat robin try to enter my home. Actually he was fighting with the fat robin he saw reflected in my window pane. He was remarkably beefy coming out of a long cold winter. But he could see only a flat dimension of existence—his reflection.

Post 2: Accept yourself. It's all right; it's acceptable to be the way we are. It may take as much as a gallon of glue to put our hearts back together. But it's o k. You may be broken-hearted. You may be bruised. You be derailed. If your wheels are a little out of round—so what! They should be. It's alright. Accept it—for now.

> *When my spirit was overwhelmed*
> *within me,*
> *then You knew my path.*
> ~ PSALMS 142-3

Post 3: Avoid labels. Labels invalidate us and diminish others. Don't let anybody label you. You know who you are. Don't label others, either. Judge not. Leave all judgment to God.

Post 4: Be steady. Be the one others may count on (not the jumping, injuring individuals, of course). Be conscientious. Be painstaking in carrying out your tasks. Show great care. Be dedicated. Be steady down the middle.

Post 5: Give service. Be of good service. Never expect service. Be gracious when and if service is given. Fully acknowledge the service provider. Engage with the provider at hand. Help others. Donate time and donate money.

Post 6: Never go along with an oppressor. Never ever accept abuse in any form. This may be a universal corner post for all of us. Understand that abuse is not normal. There are varying degrees of abuse, of course, but abuse is abuse. No exceptions. But please understand the following:

In the animal world aggression is common—for a reason. Animal aggression is distinct. It is formed for protection of young, protection of territory, and protection of a food supply. It is predictable within each species. There is intra-species comfort within this predictability. It is not abuse. There is a distinction.

In the natural world, survival and evolution is absolute. If it weren't that way the species would wither and weaken anyway. Savor and understand nature. Apply it to your own life and well-being.

But in the human world abuse is not normal. Forgive and forget, but never go along.

"Forgiveness is giving up the hope that the past could have been any different."
~ OPRAH WINFREY[9]

Post 7: Avoid the injuring party if necessary. Avoid being the target of abuse. Avoid your own painful attachment to abuse. Minimize contact with any and all abusers. Disengage from the injuring source, no matter the cost.

Relationship problems, like most emotional struggles, represent a major drain on your health and well-being, so be ruthless in cutting any unhealthy relationships from your life.
~ JOSEPH MERCOLA D O[10]
ARTICLES.MERCOLA.COM
2.23.2013

---

[9] Oprah Winfrey, "The Oprah Winfrey Show." CBS, TV, no date given.

[10] Joseph Mercola, articles.mercola.com, 2.23.201. About 15 percent of the population has psychotic, anti-social personality disorders. When you are in a relationship with one of these people, you will feel emotionally fatigued and upset, recurrently. If you notice these signs, ditch the relationship, and that may include a family member, friend, employer, etc.

Before we proceed with more posts it may be necessary to install a few rails to keep our fence upright and steady, particularly if we are feeling a little wobbly.

Fence rails to consider and install:

Select from the following, to consider and to stabilize your selected posts:

- Don't get caught in the old trap of trying to please the unreachable individual(s). Remember that person may be in a different part of the spiritual journey. That's another journey, not yours, anymore.

- Take the geographic cure if necessary. You and your inner child walk away, wave goodbye. You are your own parent now. Establish long distances, if necessary, both physical and emotional.

- Protect yourself. Eliminate the abuser from your life, entirely, if necessary. Sever all ties or just set limits. Talk about the weather, only the weather...this is hard.

- Don't let the injuring party occupy one more brain cell of your time.

- Emotionally detach when and if you can.

- Replace your established standards of reaction to abuse.

Silence is sometimes the best answer.
~ THE DALAI LAMA

Find a new family if necessary. It may be necessary. Spend more time around people who are conventional. This will open a vast spiritual door.

Remember, you are not alone. There are a whole bunch of us out there.

There are more posts to install:

Post 8: Avoid triggers of any type, any stimulus that sets you off. Take inventory of your personal triggers. Triggers are costly. They backfire—mostly backfire.

For example, fatigue is a trigger for some of us. List two triggers here:

_____

_____

Do you have dual triggers? Identify two dual triggers here:

_____

_____

Post 9: Avoid toxic, troublesome attractions. Stay away from toxic people in your life. Trouble may be familiar. In old time familiarity we might find trouble and troublesome people attractive. They may also be dangerous.

Danger and dangerous people may be familiar so danger offers more attraction to the adult child in us. Stay away from dangerous environments. You must stay away. This is a survival rule.

> Beware of false prophets, who come to you
> in sheep's clothing...
> ~ MATTHEW 7:15

Was Matthew describing a 21st century personality disorder? I wonder.

Post 10: Stay risk-averse. Learn to love safety and live safely. Avoid the jungle. Don't jump into anything you are not prepared for. Get off any edge upon which you may be living, working, playing or traveling.

Post 11: Keep yourself intact. Plant this post and protect yourself. Defend yourself. Communicate directly and honestly with others. It took a lot of time and healing to get to this place. So hold on.

Post 12: Set a high value on yourself. Hold tight to your value. Explain your value to others. Display your value. Focus on the task at hand, determine your direction, and then set out on a course of action.

Post 13: Don't let your mind wander. It is the nature of our mind to wander. Traumatized people relive events over and over as if they were in the present, intruding into the daily waking state like a ditty or a song that we can't get out of our head. Try this: "Twitter" to yourself to be here now.

Keep your mind close to the task at hand.

Remember mindfulness.

All is to be brought,
as an act of faith,
to the moment of Now.
No part of our self can be left separate.
~ TURBULANCE IN THE RIVER
AUTHOR MICHAEL SAWAYA, ATTORNEY

Engage in continuous self-awareness to keep you mentally in the present.

There is nowhere else to be.

Replace the caustic events stored in your active memory. Mentally post status notes to yourself. Identify current conditions.

More rails to consider and set:

Select from the following, and then set them as rails between your posts. Think of your rails as your stabilizers:

- Describe yourself to yourself. Describe your environment and your current activity to yourself in three sentences or fewer. Look around and describe:

  _____
  _____
  _____

- Be here. Erase your old story-tapes. Stop and/or reduce multitasking. Stay focused on the task at hand, one task at a time. Call out the task at hand:

  _____

- Find a routine to your life, your own unique rhythm. Practice that routine throughout your day. For example, make the bed after you drink your morning drink. Make each effort part of a daily practiced rhythm.

- Write down snippets of your life as it is today. This will keep you present:

_____

_____

_____

- Replace the old tapes in your head, the co-presence of the formative family in your brain. Remind yourself what you are doing and where you are right now.

- Create a new dimension to float over your whole life, a co-presence with yourself; ping-pong co-present messages to yourself until the old negative tapes stop.

STOP.

STOP.

STOP.

STOP.

They will stop

Write down what you are doing right here, right now. This is what exists:

_____

_____

_____

- Become intimate with yourself, your true self. Spend time alone. Spend some time alone every day. Remind yourself of who you are. Describe yourself to yourself:

_____

_____

_____

- Get rooted. Get grounded. Develop a sense of place. Get to know birds, seasons, weather and the land. Develop a bone-deep knowledge of place and how the light changes and other keen observations. Note your observations:

_____

_____

_____

That's enough. Enough is enough. Celebrate what you have over what you do not have—or what you think you should have.

Post 14: Pray. Prayer is worth it. Nothing can take heaven from you. Heaven is assured. Heaven is your birthright. This life on earth is God's gift to you. This is your preparation for heaven and for the afterlife.
If you don't know how to pray, start big. Pray the words of protection from the *Lorica of Patrick of Ireland* (see page 91). Patrick wrote these words around 377 AD. You may adapt them to your own personal situation. I think of Patrick's prayer as a comfort and a guide.

Jesus, of course, taught us how to pray:

"When you pray, go into your room, and when you have shut your door, pray to your Father who is in the secret place; and your Father who sees in secret will reward you openly."
~ MATTHEW 6:6

Post 15: Expect change. Make God your partner in your earthly life, in everything you do. Ask God for each change you want in your life. I usually ask for just one change at a time, so I may keep track.

For your Father knows the things you have need of before you ask Him.
~ MATTHEW 6:8

Our prayers rise immediately to the heart of God. I find I get what I request...in due time.

Be careful what you ask for! Select from the following then set them up as rails between posts:

- Ask God to guide you in your choices.
- Ask God to support you in your goals.
- Ask God to direct you in your goal-making path
- Ask God to accompany you in your spiritual journey.
- Ask God to help you to carry out only the work of God.

And Jabez called on the God of Israel saying, "Oh, that You would bless me indeed, and enlarge my territory, that Your hand would be with me, and that You Would keep me from evil, that I may not cause pain."
~ 1CHRONICLES 4:10

God is tenacious.

God will be there for you.

God will take care of you.

God will heal you.

God loves you.

God will release you.

Just ask.

> *You did not choose Me, but I chose you.*
> ~ JOHN 15:16

This is sooo powerful!

Understand this:

God chose you.

You have it on Authority.

Post 17: Spiritual Solidarity. Acknowledge your real family. There is spiritual solidarity amongst all the children of God, even the oppressed.

> *So we, being many, are one body in Christ, and individually members of one another.*
> ~ ROMANS 12:5

Every action done by one is profitable to all.

There is one body and one Spirit,
just as you were called in one hope of
your calling;
one Lord, one faith, one baptism;
one God and Father of all, who is
above all, and through all, and in you all.
~ EPHESIANS 4:4-6

Reach for the global connection that weaves us together. If you were baptized you are members of a community. This is your family. Find it. Hold fast to it. Gather other souls around you.

For by one spirit we were all baptized
into one body—whether Jews or Greeks,
whether slaves or free—and have all been
made to drink into one Spirit.
for in fact the body is not one member
but many.
~ 1CORINTHIANS 12:13, 14

This is a vast concept, central to well-being. It has a corporate nature—this life.
And it offers continuity to our afterlife.

This is a tall order, but it is also a generous gift from God. This gift of soul survival offers deep comfort to us in this life.

Post 18: Don't resent the success of others. Stay close to your loving friends.

Let your conduct be without covetousness,
and be content with such things as
you have. For he Himself has said, "I
will never leave you nor forsake you."
~ HEBREWS 13:5

We are told that friendships help us prolong our life. This is good. We need a long life to learn to fulfill our ultimate purpose.

Friends offer social support. They offer a distinct break from family discord and other forms of discord. We have a really good time when we are with our friends. Friends are important. They help us process the truth.

> Friendships can educate us to what life is,
> or what life may become.
> Friendships are mirrors of our true self.

Post 19: Connect deeply to others through work and play every day. Out of your suffering you have expert knowledge of what should not happen, what should not be and what you should not do. Your instinct is well-informed.

More rails to consider installing:

Assist where you are needed.

Facilitate healing in others.

Give back more than you take.

Reach out.

Post 20: Be a caregiver.

> *For you, brethren, have been called to liberty; only do not use liberty as an opportunity for the flesh, but through love serve one another.*
> ~ GALATIANS 5:13

When you feel love and know love, you have discovered meaning in life now and into your future. Love provides guidance to your daily living.

Post 21: Practice gratitude. Each night as you fall asleep review your day for everything and everyone you hold in thanksgiving.

More cross rails:

Count your blessings.
Find the blessing in each day.

This exercise, the blessing exercise, is the secret to deep happiness. It will establish a tight foundation for your well-being. It will drop you into peaceful sleep.

Post 22: Be grateful to others who have helped you, too. Express your gratitude.

> *It is in the Realm of Gratitude that we discover who we are; and it is in that Realm that Love, our Creator, connects with us, listens to our intentions and supports us in the directions that we take.*
> ~ TURBULANCE IN THE RIVER
> MICHAEL SAWAYA

Post 23: Cull old grief. If grief and old troubles continue to intrude in the present, cull them out. Gather them together and remove them from your heart.

Let them go.
Identify old stories and send them packing—forever.

Yes, it happened. Yes, it happened to you. But don't let old grief sit on top of you.

The past is dead.
Let it go.

*Weeping may endure for a night
but joy comes in the morning.*
~ PSALMS 30:5

Let the past be the past as if it was somebody else's story...

"...and their sin I will remember no more."
~ JEREMIAH 3:34

Post 24: Visualize a future, your own future. Think about available information and resources to achieve your goals and dreams.

Post 25: Leave a bad situation. If all else fails, then "get out of Dodge," leave a bad or dangerous situation. Take the geographic cure if necessary. Move if you must.

Jesus advised his followers...

*"Do not give what is holy to the dogs,
nor cast your pearls before swine, lest
they trample them under their feet, and
turn and tear you in pieces."*
~ MATTHEW 7:6

Post 26: Research everything. Study; read; acquire more knowledge. Knowledge is the key to success. Get a general education, a pathway to success. Reach for high scholastic achievement.

Post 27: Get an education in your field. Educate your precious inner child. Get a degree and/or the maximum certifications in your field. Learn everything that will assist you in your personal and professional growth.

Excel at what you do.

Post 28: Work hard. Work very, very hard, harder than your peers. The value of work is not only in material gains but in its keen distraction from our negative feelings and the old tapes in your head. Work engages us in meaningful activity.

Not lagging in diligence, fervent in spirit, serving the Lord.
~ ROMANS 12:11

Post 29: Spoil yourself. Take time out to enjoy yourself. All of life does not have to be goal directed. Love God then do as you please.

Top rail: Find an inner source of joy.

A merry heart does good, like medicine.
~ PROVERBS 17:22

Middle rail: Treat yourself, often.

But he who is of a merry heart has a continual feast.
~ PROVERBS 15:15

Lower rail: Do all you ever wanted to do, always mindful of safety; never get yourself in trouble.

You have a house with a fence around it!

Congratulations!

That's a fence!

No one and nothing can step over it.
You have to let them in.

No, No, Not Sleep

No, no, not sleep

Not now

Not when I am this happy!

Chapter 7

Decorate
Your Fresh Heart

Delight yourself.

Be cheerful

Gravitate toward environments that suit you.

Circle what you want to do today.

Then get lost in your choices.

Focus on what you love in life.

Visit the zoo.

Go camping.

Attend a lecture.

Hike in the forest.

Climb a mountain.

Climb a tree.

Throw a party.

Dance.

Walk.

Spin.

Eat Chocolate.

Run a marathon.

Rescue a dog or a cat.

Study yoga.

Learn a new sport.

Look into a dog's eyes and see a tiny heart, an individuated heart.

Do something easy today: Go shopping.

Cook something.

Bake cookies.

Tell jokes.

Learn a new joke.

Pray.

Sit Still.

Smile at yourself.

Smile often.

Go somewhere new.

Show interest in a stranger.

Talk to the check-out person.

Study stars.

Study constellations.

Learn something new today.

Learn a craft.

Study human faces; make eye contact.

Plant a tree, a maple tree. Fall color is enough to live for.

*'Your life
shall be as a prize to you, because you
have put your trust in Me.' says the
Lord.*
~ JEREMIAH 39:18

Write down what you would like to do, to observe this very day:

_____

_____

_____

_____

_____

_____

May you be content with yourself just the
way you are.
~ TERESA OF AVILA

Examples:

Love light, the color of light and the seasonal changes in natural light. Anticipate light shifts. Wait for the gray light of November to end and the golden light of February to arrive, February 10 to be exact (in Colorado). It always returns. There's a lesson in this phenomenon.

Observe growth and changes in plants noting their pre-season colors, the shift to pre-bud stage, the bud, the color, and the growth into leaf, flower and fruit.
Listen to silence, the silence of an empty room, the snap of a radiator, the whistle of a far-off train.

Listen to birds calling for a mate, giving warning, identifying a food source, or simply gathering in song. Listen for the distinction.

Enjoy scents, the whiff of blooms, the lack of scent and the soft subtle after-bloom, the almost not-here scents of flower, vine, weed and herb.

Retain the glint of light on snow. (My mind combines glint with the red twig willow above winter mud.) Enjoy the combinations in nature.

Note skies of every color. Yes, even green.

Watch waters of every mood from playful to somber, from busy to tired.

Enjoy music, lying in bed listening to the words of show tunes, enjoying concepts and impressions of other human beings.

Enjoy relationships with friends and colleagues. Honor associates at work. Respect and delight in them.

Bake cookies.

Walk a dog.

Pet a cat as it purrs.

Write down your delights:

_____
_____
_____
_____
_____
_____

Chapter 8

Open the Door
and
Let the Light
in

Find your balance.

Find your balance, your own unique source of balance. The universe is in balance. It has to be or it would collapse upon itself. So tap into the balance in the universe and let the light of the universe get in. Connect with the balance in the universe and inside yourself, through music, through nature or in your relationship with God.

> *Since we are receiving a*
> *kingdom which cannot be shaken, let us*
> *have grace, by which we may serve God*
> *acceptably with reverence and Godly fear.*
> ~ HEBREWS 12:28

Select a passion then dream on it. File that passion into your future. Plan it. Build a binder or a scrapbook of your dreams.

Tear out photos of places you want to visit, favorite clothes, furniture, gardens. Organize pictures of friends.

Now use your binder to remind you of your path. You have created files for your hopes and dreams. Make those dreams come true.
Join an inspirational group in person or electronically. Actively seek out relationships.

Your relationships should be fair, both personal and professional. Look for companionship and respect in all relationships. (A friend is not someone who exposes your differences and shortcomings. And a friend is not someone who compares you to others.)

Be respectful. Look for empathy from others and interact with one another in the long term. Operate from the core benefits of your relationships. This is a platform, a large part of getting balance and retaining balance.

Balance also requires responsibility: be responsible and responsive. Don't tune out or shut down.

Let the light in. Be light in your being.

Love others. It always gets back to this. Love feeds union. Love connects. It does not separate.

Love may be a hard start for you. Start simply by offering care, kindness and patience. Remember our early exercise to look at others with love in your eyes? Try it today.

Love is care.

Perhaps care is the highest form of love.
Take care of others--no negotiations. Give care freely.

Let the light in.
Then
Be the light.

*It is during our darkest moments
we must focus to see the light.*
~ ARISTOTLE

You thought you were an oak tree,
High on a hill
Ready to break.

        In fact you are a willow
        Nurtured by the banks
        Resilient
        From pressures of life.

Life Is Light

When you hear a bird song, use it as your cue.

You were born with happiness and goodness in your heart.
You were made in the image and the likeness of God.

This is your song.

For every house is built by someone,
but He who built all things is God.
~ HEBREWS 3:4

Lorica
of
Patrick of Ireland[11]

I arise today
Through a mighty strength the invocation of the Trinity,
Through a belief in the Threeness,
Through confession of the Oneness
Of the Creator of creation.

I arise today
Through the strength of Christ's birth and His baptism
Through the strength of His crucifixion and His burial.

Through the strength of His resurrection and his Ascension
Through the strength of His descent for the judgment of doom.

I arise today
Through the strength of the love of cherubim,
In obedience of angels,
In service of archangels,
The hope of resurrection to meet with reward,
In the prayers of patriarchs,
In preaching of the apostles,
In faiths of confessors,
In innocence of virgins,
In deeds of righteous men.

I arise today
Through the strength of heaven
Light of sun,

Splendor of fire,
Speed of lightning,
Swiftness of the wind,
Depth of sea,
Stability of earth,
Firmness of rock.

---

[11] A "Lorica" is body armor. Consider this is a prayer of protection.

I arise today
Through God's strength to pilot me;
God's might to uphold me,
God's wisdom to guide me,
God's eye to look before me,

God's ear to hear me,
God's word to speak for me,
God's hand to guard me,
God's way to lie before me,
God's shield to protect me,
God's hosts to save me
From snares of the devil,
From temptations of vices,
From everyone who desires me ill,
Afar and a near,
Alone or in multitude.

I summon today all these powers
Between me and evil.
Against every cruel merciless power that opposes my body and soul.

Against incantations of false prophets,
Against black laws of pagandom,
Against false laws of heretics,
Against craft of idolatry,
Against spells of wizards,
Against every knowledge that corrupts man's body and soul

Christ shield me today
Against poison,
Against burning,
Against wounding,
Against drowning,
So that reward may come to me in abundance.

Christ with me, Christ before me, Christ behind me,
Christ in me, Christ beneath me, Christ above me,
Christ on my right, Christ on my left,
Christ when I lie down, Christ when I sit down,
Christ in the heart of every man who thinks of me,
Christ in the mouth of every man who speaks of me,
Christ in the eye that sees me,
Christ in the ear that hears me.

I arise today
Through a mighty strength,
The invocation of the Trinity,
Through a belief in the Threeness,
Through confession of the oneness
Of the Creator of creation.

PATRICK OF IRELAND

Final Thoughts

As I write, the front page of our daily newspaper reports the suicide-double suicide pact of twin girls. They were acting out of empathy with the victims of the Columbine Massacre that occurred in 1999. It is puzzling. I am aghast.

I am sensitive to the orphan aspect of an adult person's child experience. The orphaned adult child is keenly visible to me, sometimes in the face of depression, sometimes in a stammer, in a stutter or a robotic stare. And I truly wonder, what happened to that stranger who was dominated simultaneously by pressing emotion and by peppered anger? Who discarded, who cast off this adult's helpless child, that little child carried around inside the adult psyche?

Should this be of public concern? Put this in context: One in four girls is sexually assaulted before the age of eighteen.[12] More than one and a half million juveniles run away or are thrown out of their homes, each year. [13] Some young ones are subjected to harrowing experiences between a lifestyle of couch-surfing and under-bridge encamp-ment. They have been pushed by circumstances to their limit, to an edge so tenuous their instability is guaranteed.

No one is looking out for them. No one comes to their rescue.[14] They are nobody's children.

---

[12] Denver Children's Advocacy Center, 7.19.2010. www.DenverCAC.org.

[13] *New York Times*, 10.26.2009

[14] Consider these statistics: the United States averages 32,000 suicides per year- 8.3 million Americans consider suicide; 2.3 million Americans plan suicide and 1.31 million attempt suicide annually. Those most likely to consider suicide are only 18-25 years of age- young adults- chronologically close-in-life to their family of origin and to their formative years. SAMHSA 9.17.2009

In our highly civilized and prosperous culture parental neglect and maltreatment still require more focus and concern particularly as it involves the deliberate devaluation of the female child.

Henrik Ibsen, a nineteenth century playwright, referred to as the "Father" of modern theatre, exposed this devastating parenting pattern in his play, "The Wild Duck." Ibsen created a female protagonist, a child protagonist, who commits suicide—to please her father!

What about boys-gone-bad who commit dangerous, even murderous, acts? We do not know the absolute cause of murder/suicide, but we can verify tumultuous family relationships and covert maltreatment of children. It is species-specific, sadly our species.

Most parents are doing the best they can. Nevertheless some parents lack empathy or the skills for parenting. Couple this with the compression of our digital age and intergenerational dispassion, maltreatment and neglect are excessively high hurdles for a young person to overcome.[15]

---

[15] Only 2% of children raised in foster homes attend college, reported by Channel 9 News Denver, Colorado 12.13.10.

Acknowledgements

My developmental assets were considerable and I was motivated. Fortunate for me I met with wide support by nonparent adults. I enjoyed an encouraging environment built on integrity and expectation within a community of peers engaged in responsible behavior. I built that support into my life. Specifically I am grateful for:

My husband: I married a knight,[16] the person I admired most in life. I trusted him and I trusted his heart. From ducks to dogs, wild horses, even a wild turkey imprinted on him. Fish gladly took his fly. I tell God how lucky I have been to have him as my love and to be loved by him. He calls himself my "cut-man, always in your corner."

My husband has been my partner guiding me through life's twists. He smoothed out warps, deviations, and prompted me that "life is a sport" and "life is wonderful."

My husband was a well-loved child. He is stable and generous. He believes in me. He encourages and appreciates my efforts in every area of our lives except one: he always wins the wishbone! I swear! I don't know how he does it.

My therapist: the other man I hold in deepest respect, in affection and in gratitude for his unerring guidance, his constancy and the depth of his understanding, a depth I have yet to tap, so wrapped in me as I have been—and to his predecessors also.

---

[16] As a young adult I chose partners with limited capacity who bore a behavioral resemblance to my family of origin—in its most devastating interaction with me. I did marry one other time. That relationship held the same emotional grip on me as my mother of origin. Once charmed, it morphed and disintegrated.

Director of Financial Aid, College of New Rochelle: a powerful positive influence: fifteen semesters of college financing, with a loan forgiveness program, a National Defense Student Loan, spurred by Nikita Khrushchev, Sputnik and The Cold War. This program was urged by President Eisenhower and forcefully backed by the then Senator John F. Kennedy.

Friends: lifelong friends, who are tender, smart, active, capable people who shared my interests and values and took the time to read this book.

No stranger to greatness and the common man, I counted among my core group of friends: a garage carpenter, contractors, landscapers, attorneys, politicians, a federal judge, farmers, irrigators, social workers, nutritionists, teachers; I counted as friends international performers, a platinum record artist, painters, fine artists, writers, other interior designers, even one Nobel Prize winner—a former US president.

Thanks to all of you for the fun, affirmations, information, pep talks and pick-me-ups. Thanks for your wide-world views, the sharing and the caring that contributed to my successes and survival. A true example was my cradle friend:

She and I never said a harsh word to each other. We did not allow our philosophical or political disagreements to become the central focus of our relationship. We operated from the core benefits of the relationship. We interacted in the long term, never in the moment only.

We were both at risk for loss of self, loss of reality, scrambled by the planet, so we really listened to each other. We identified our truth. I nurtured her and she nurtured me. Throughout our long lives this mutual loyalty and constancy has helped us absorb the recurring impossible pain of our difficult childhoods.

Clients: a coincidental cluster in the 1990's dragged me back to Christianity. You were right. I am grateful. Thank you.

The Public Library: I read every book in the children's section and I returned every one too. As a child I lost myself in the library. I consistently use the public library even today.

The old *Philadelphia Art Museum* with its historic furniture galleries braced my instincts as a designer and increased my appetite for the design trade.

Dr. Theatre: It was make believe. As actress, director and set designer I could be who I wanted to be. I could assemble or dismantle the world as I wished it.

Religious Orders: The Orders remained faithful and passionate about building schools and colleges to educate and shape women.

A high-country gene base: downhill skiing, swimming in hot springs, jogging through city parks, hiking in mountains, riding horses while listening to a birdcall symphony, searching silently for big game and inhaling majestic views. I could not live without mountain sports, a big breakout that kept me from staying dazed and destroyed.

All these and they and them I acknowledge as opportunities. I grasped them and employed them to source my foundation and build deep footers.

Biophilia: experiences of nature applicable to everyday life aiding adaptation. I observed:
~ Trout do not live in slack water.
~ Trout live in the feed line in holding areas—out of the sun.
~ Ducks have everything they need.
~ A blue moon, twice, month after month, 1983.
~ A silvery moonrise over the mountain lights-up grass after dark.
~ Cold stone lowers ambient temperature.
~ There is a hatch on the river when the swallows swarm.
~ Two butterflies fight over a single flower in a field of flowers.
~ Brown trout chew live trout, eat fingerlings and newly laid eggs; cow-elk abandon their young; a five pound cat eat a full-grown squirrel; coyotes roam in packs— seven deep; vultures strip a dead horse to the bone in a single day; turkeys line-up to gangbang dead hens.
I learned:
~ Rams (bucks) kill young lambs, even their offspring.
~ Male crocodiles eat croc hatchlings.
~ Bears kill ten percent of a protected flock of sheep in a single summer.
~ Giraffes compete by breaking one another's bones.
As I watch:
~ Deer share the raising of newborn twin fawns.
~ Geese re-pattern themselves through safe flights, clear of hunters and predators.
~ Leaves fall to the ground, so what.

It is the way it is.

Recommended Resources and Reading

Resources

Rape, Abuse and Incest National Network, www.rainn.org. The organization offers online and telephone support 1/800 656-HOPE (4673)

Recommended Reading

Agatston, MD, Arthur, *The South Beach Diet*, The Delicious, Doctor-Designed, Foolproof Plan for Fast and Healthy Weight Loss, N Y: Rodale, 2003. Agatston offers a guide to glycemic index meal planning, with proven results for weight loss and cardiovascular health.
ISBN 1-57954-646-3

Alexander, MD, Eben, *Proof of Heaven, A Neurosurgeon's Journey into the Afterlife*, NY: Simon and Schuster, 2012. An academic neurosurgeon explains life after death based on his near death experience.
ISBN 978-1-4516-9519-9

Crowley, Chris & Henry S. Lodge, MD, *Younger Next Year, A Guide to Living like 50 until You're 80 and Beyond,* NY: Workman Publishing, 2004. This is an information-packed book teaching us to live life with renewed vitality, physically, emotionally, and mentally.
ISBN 0-7611-3423-9

Dalai Lama, His Holiness The, and Howard C. Cutler, MD, *The Art of Happiness, A Handbook for Living,* N Y: Riverhead Books, 1998. Cutler explains that happiness is to want what we have, that happiness is an achievable goal.
ISBN 1-57322-111-2

Gleser, Robert A., *The Health Mark Program for Life,* NY: McGraw Hill Book Company, 1988. Gleser offers a baseline program on healthy eating and healthy living; written by a prominent Denver physician.
ISBN 0-07-023494-9

Goleman, Daniel, *Emotional Intelligence: Why it can matter more than IQ*, NY: Bantam Books, 1998. Goleman provides insights into mastery of human behavior to benefit our lives.
ISBN 0-553-37506-7

Grimm, The Brothers, *Grimms' Fairy Tales,* Chicago: MA Donahue & Company. A collection of classic household stories puts parental behaviors in humanistic historic context.

Holy Bible, Scripture taken from The New King James Version. Nashville: Thomas Nelson Publishers, 1982.

Johnson, Elizabeth A, *Truly Our Sister*: *A Theology of Mary in the Communion of Saints,* NY: Continuum, 2006. Johnson's deep theological study of Mary, the mother of Jesus, is transferred to her role as model and companion.
ISBN 0-8264-1827-9

Jones, E Stanley, *The Way,* NY: Abingdon-Cokesbury Press, 1946. This book is dialectic on the Christian experience.

Kullberg, Kelley Monroe, *Finding God at Harvard: Spiritual Journeys of Thinking Christians*, Downers Grove: Inter Varsity Press, 1996. Accessible arguments and investigations for the Christian faith are presented by the Harvard University community of scholars.
ISBN 0030834338

Machiavelli, Niccolo, *The Prince,*_NY: EP Dutton, 1908. Machiavelli's historic observations offer a surprising insight into the world the way it is.

Mack, MD, John E and Rita S Rogers, MD, *The Alchemy of Survival: One Woman's Journey,* Reading, Mass: Addison Wesley Publishing Company, 1988. A survivor of the Holocaust offers lessons on fortitude and hope in extreme conditions.
ISBN 0-201-12682-6

Moore, Thomas, *Care of the Soul: A Guide for Cultivating Depth and Sacredness in Everyday Life*, NY: Harper Perennial, 1940. This is an impressive guide to the details of soul re-connection, cultivation and grace.
ISBN 0-06-092224-9

Muller, Wayne. *Legacy of the Heart*: *Spiritual Advantages of a Painful Childhood*, NY: Simon and Shuster, 1992. "We want to convince our parents to apologize, to love us, and to make right what was done so horribly wrong...Let what is true be true: We were hurt." This statement by the author calls it out. He goes on to explain our vulnerability makes us more open to our experience of God.
ISBN 0671-79784 0

Muller, Wayne. *Sabbath: Finding Rest, Renewal, and Delight in our Busy Lives*, NY: Bantam Books, 1999. "The gifts of grace and delight are present and abundant; the time to live and love and give thanks and rest and delight is now, this moment, this day." What a gracious way of living. Thank you.
ISBN 0-553-38011 7

Peck, Scott. *People of the Lie: The Hope for Healing Human Evil*, NY: Touchstone, 1983. From the perspective of his Christian commitment Peck identifies evil as the root of human failure.
ISBN 0 7126 1857 0

Quindlen, Anna, *A Short Guide to a Happy Life*, NY: Random House, 2000. Precious moments are examined and revisited teaching us to love the journey our life offers.
ISSBN 0-375-50461-3

Roth, Kimberlee and Freda Fiedman, *Surviving a Borderline Parent: How to Heal Your Childhood Wounds & Build Trust, Boundaries and Self-Esteem*, New Harbinger Publications, 2003. The authors identify a cluster problem, bi-polar disorder, and offer solutions to change the life of the adult child of a BPD parent.
ISBN 1-57224-328-7

Sanders, Jennifer, *Wear More Cashmere: 151 Ways to Pamper Your Inner Princess,* Gloucester, Massachusetts: Fair Winds Press, 2003. This book offers gentle, playful suggestions to help lead a life of calmness and luxury.
ISBN: 1-921412-34-0

Sawaya, Michael, *Turbulence in the River: Restoring your Spiritual Birthright*, Denver: The Observant Press, 2011. Sawaya taps into profound mysticism in the form of a Spirit Guide teaching us to connect the spirit world with our own psychology as we journey through the universes. This is an articulate treatise on human life in relation to our Creator. In addition he explains the structure of "Love" and the elements of the universes.
ISBN-13; 978-0-615-28714-0

Warren, Richard, *The Purpose Driven Life*, Grand Rapids, Michigan: Zondervan, 2002. This is a work book, grounded in Pastor Warren's firm belief that God has a plan for each of us, and to know and understand that plan is our mission.
ISBN 0-310-20571-9

Wilkerson, Dr. Bruce A. and David Kopf, *The Prayer of Jabez*: *Breaking Through to the Blessed Life,* The Break Through Series, Colorado Springs: Waterbrook Multnomah Publishers Inc., 2000. Based on lessons from the Book of Chronicles we learn God is faithful to those who seek Him. Wilkerson entreats us to do a little more than what is required.
ISBN 978-159024831

About the Book

This book will impact your life for the better. It will teach you how you can recover from a dysfunctional family, from child abuse, from emotional abuse, from neglect, from abusive ongoing relationships. It will enlighten you on self-help strategies—simple exercises to manage depression and anxiety.

An earthy self-help handbook, merged in spirituality and collective wisdom, developed from the author's personal experience: a step by step strategy to repair the soul of the young child that each adult carries deep inside, to find well-being and to thrive in happy, healthy independence.

Learn to:
- Calm your inner child
- Quiet down your anxiety and depression.
- Set boundaries
- Free yourself from frustration and abuse
- Connect deeply with others
- Heal yourself
- Overcome loneliness
- Find balance

Transform your life into:
- A reinvention of your former self
- An artisan lifestyle
- A spirit journey

You can get results.
You can move through defenses and set them aside by active living.
Anxiety and depression recede into the wings.

Advance Praise for **Sweep Away Your Thorny Childhood**

"Leave all those nagging memories behind and use this easy guide to go forward with comfort and pride."

"Tired of those my way or the highway self-help books? Now we have an easy to read, comforting route to leave self-doubt and hurtful memories on the side of the road and travel on—enjoying the wonderful highway of life."

"Is your smothered spirituality longing for a way to shine? Read this book and learn how to let it emerge and become a part of your daily life."
~ RICHARD N. WITTKOPP. CARPENTER.

"I was floored by this book, rich in metaphor. I've copied phrases from this book to have on hand."
~ JANICE SIMPSON, MD. ADOLESCENT PSYCHIATRIST.

"There are an awful lot of people who could be helped by this book. It is earth shattering stuff--so enjoyable to read-- not heavy. It's a nice blend."
~ BARBARA MUNSON. MUNSON COMMUNICATIONS.

"If everyone did this stuff, wouldn't we have a nicer world?"
~ JULIA JOHNSON. INTERIOR DESIGNER.

"I love this workbook for EVERYONE. Knowledge is power and I hope the knowledge of the Word that you used with precision touches peoples' lives."
~ LAURA LARSON. SPIRITUAL FREEDOM CHURCH, SCOTTSDALE, ARIZONA.

"It's beautiful."
~ HAL WAKEFIELD, MD. PSYCHIATRIST.

"You've got to learn to take care of yourself because no one will do it for you. Your future happiness depends on you."
~ ZU LEMA LOPEZ-OREJEL AGE 17. SOUTHWEST EARLY COLLEGE, DENVER, COLORADO.

About the Author

Sandra Elizabeth Clinger is an award-winning internationally recognized interior designer. Her design work appears in over fifty publications and may be seen on HGTV. Ms Clinger is a former therapist who specialized in abnormal development. She holds a BA degree from the College of New Rochelle and an MA degree from Villanova University. Today she is a member of the American Society of Interior Designers and is recognized by the National Association of Home Builders as a Certified Active Adult Housing Specialist. Despite a medical diagnosis of PTSD generated in her formative years, she enjoys a long, sweet marriage and a rewarding career. She holds multiple professional distinctions including a national first place award for Historic Preservation and a Colorado Home of the Year Award. She is a Lange Ski Boot poster model and hostess to former President Carter and Mrs. Carter.

Ms Clinger lives in Colorado with her husband in a house with a fence around it.

Photo by David Alan Clinger

Summary and Conclusion

Sweep Away Your Thorny Childhood is a self-help handbook, employing the analogy of home building, to find well-being and to thrive in happy and healthy independence.

It is merged in spirituality and collective wisdom, developed from the author's personal experience of surviving the depths of a disturbing childhood.

The workbook offers eight step by step strategies to repair the soul of the young child that each adult carries deep inside.

Join the conversation and community at:
www.sweep-away.com
www.linkedin.com/in/sweepawayyourthornychildhood
https://www.facebook.com/pages/Well-Being-Center/

Notes